THE PUMPKIN COOKBOOK

THE
PUMPKIN
COOKBOOK

HAMLYN

First published in 1998
by Hamlyn
a division of Octopus Publishing Group Ltd
2-4 Heron Quays, London E14 4JP
This edition published 2001
Copyright © 1998, 2001 Octopus Publishing Group Ltd

ISBN 0 600 60518 3

Printed in China

Senior Editor: Sasha Judelson
Editor: Barbara Horn
Commissioning Editor: Nicola Hill

Art Director: Keith Martin
Executive Art Editor: Mark Winwood
Designer: Norma Martin

Production Controller: Melanie Frantz

Photo credits: Mary Evans Picture Library: 5, 8,
12, 18, 22, 25, 32, 36, 38, 40, 44, 48, 52, 57
Reed International Books Ltd. /Nick Carmen: 2/3, 23, 27,
39, /Jeremy Hopley: endpapers, 7, 11, 43, 51, 55, 59,
63, /Diana Miller: 15/Allan Rosenberg: 35, 47, /Clive Streeter: 31

Notes
1 Use whole milk unless otherwise stated.
2 Use sweet (unsalted) butter unless otherwise stated.
3 Use medium-size vegetables unless otherwise stated.

Contents

Pumpkins

The Versatile Vegetable

Pumpkins, piled high in the market and on roadside stalls, used to decorate store windows and accessorize fashion photography, make their appearance as the leaves begin to turn and fall, heralding the arrival of Halloween and reminding us that Thanksgiving is on the way. Indeed, some people think of this icon of fall only in terms of jack-o'-lanterns and pumpkin pie. Yet here is a truly extraordinary vegetable, not only in terms of the size it can achieve, but also because of its versatility, for it is one of the few foods that can delight the palate throughout a meal, as soup and in salad, as main course or side dish, and in a variety of hot and cold desserts.

History The pumpkin is one of the oldest known vegetables. Seeds dating back to 7000–5500 B.C. have been found in Mexico, and there is evidence that several varieties were being cultivated in tropical and subtropical areas of the Americas at least as far back as 3000 B.C. The Spanish conquistadors returning from the New World introduced the pumpkin, as well as the potato, to Europe in the sixteenth century, but it did not flourish as well in the cooler climate and was used mainly as animal fodder until recent times. Today the pumpkin is grown throughout the world, particularly in New England, New Jersey and Florida in this country, and also in Australia, Central Africa, parts of Russia, the Balkans and Southeast Asia.

Pumpkin and squash varieties The pumpkin is a member of the Curcurbitaceae, or gourd, family, which includes gourds, melons, cucumbers and summer and winter squashes. Because pumpkin and some varieties of squash share certain botanical classifications, the names are often used interchangeably, leading to not a little confusion.

The name squash is derived from the Algonguian *isquoutersquashes* and the closely related *askútasquash* used by the Narragansetts; the word in both languages means "eaten raw," which indicates that it may first have been applied to the type we refer to as summer squash. These thin-skinned varieties, such as zucchini, pattypan and crookneck, are picked before they are ripe and are intended for immediate consumption, while those we call winter squash, such as acorn, butternut and Hubbard, are harvested when fully ripe and have good storage qualities.

Although many people use the name pumpkin loosely for many types of winter squash, we usually apply it only to those varieties with a yellow or orange, hard, grooved rind; stems that are generally firmer, more ridged and squarer than those of other winter squash; and a strongly flavored orange coloured flesh. Pumpkins vary in shape from round to oblong, and in size from less than 4 lb to more than 200 lb.

Many of the cultivars have names that reflect their size, where they are grown or a seasonal association, particularly Halloween. Among the small cultivars, for example, which grow up to 4 ½ lb, there is Jack Be Little, Baby Pam, and Munchkin, as well as Spookie and Trick-or-Treat. Medium-size pumpkins, ranging from 4 ½–25 lb, include Hallowe'en, Connecticut Field, Jack-o'Lantern and Triple Treat. Large pumpkins, such as Funnyface, Ghost Rider, and Big Max, are between 26 and 220 lb, while the world record for the largest pumpkin is 821 lb for an Atlantic Giant.

Cultivation All pumpkins, like most winter squashes, grow on long trailing vines with compound tendrils and large round or heart-shaped, prickly leaves. Despite their thick-skinned appearance, these are very tender plants, particularly sensitive to cold, so sowing has to wait for settled warm weather. Then the seeds can be planted directly into hills or trenches of slightly acid soil at intervals of 2 ½–3 feet in rows 8–12 feet apart. The plants produce both female and male flowers, but only the latter have pollen. For a fruit to develop, the pollen must be transferred by bees to the female flowers. However, since each female flower is open for pollination for only one day, many flowers do not produce pumpkins. Pumpkins are fully matured about four months after planting and can be stored in a dry place at 39–50°F for several months.

Cooking Pumpkin flesh can be boiled, steamed or baked. For any kind of chutney, jam or relish that you plan to keep, the pumpkin must be cooked using the pressure canning method. Consult your manual to ensure that the specified quantity of pumpkin is cooked for long enough to remove acidity. Pumpkin has a sweetish, nutty flavor which may be enhanced with herbs, cheese or spices. Freshly grated nutmeg is excellent with mashed pumpkin. Cooked pumpkin has a high water content and is therefore very low in calories — only about 75 calories in an average serving. Pumpkin is rich in vitamin A and a good source of vitamin C and potassium. The seeds of the pumpkin are high in phosphorous and potassium, and provide protein, iron, zinc, and vitamin A.

Pumpkins, Folklore and Traditions

Cinderella There are numerous versions of the tale of Cinderella, but the one written by the French poet Charles Perrault in the mid-seventeenth century is perhaps the best known. His is a fairy tale about the transformation of Cinderella from household drudge to princess. It may not have taken a great stretch of imagination for Perrault to make her fairy godmother change Cinderella's rags into a fine ball gown with a wave of her wand, but who knows by what stroke of genius he decided to transform the pumpkin, then a food for livestock, into a carriage of gold and crystal. Certainly the deep golden to orange colour and sometimes amazing size of this humble vegetable may have caught his eye. Perhaps the rotund shape with its ridges and central stem suggested a carriage with a peaked roof, and the large leaves and many tendrils reminded him of ornate ornamental carvings. We will probably never know, but we can thank him for one of the most abiding memories of childhood.

The Fairy changing Cinderella's Kitchen dress into a beautiful Ball dress.

Halloween To most Americans the pumpkin is a traditional symbol of Halloween. Even before we are old enough to carve our own jack-o'-lanterns, we depict them in our Halloween pictures with black cats, witches, and ghosts, and we tape replicas cut out of orange paper or orange card to the windows.

To understand this association we need to look back more than 2,000 years to the origins of Halloween itself. To the Celtic people, who then lived in what is now Great Britain, Ireland and northern France, October 31 was the last day of the year. It marked the end of summer and its fruitfulness, and the beginning of winter, when even the Sun seemed to be dying, leaving the world cold, dark and decaying. It was on this night, therefore, that the people honored their god of death, Samhain. They extinguished their hearth fires, leaving their homes cold and dark, symbolically imitating the pattern of nature, and congregated at the sacred bonfires built by the

Druids, their priests and leaders. After their celebrations, each family carried home a torch from the bonfire to relight its own fire, symbolizing the new year and the renewal of life, and perhaps to scare away evil spirits and light the way for ghosts, the souls of the dead, who, they believed, Samhain permitted to return to Earth for this one night.

After the Romans conquered the Celts in A.D. 43, their own festivals to honor the dead, and Pomona, their goddess of fruit trees, were combined with the Celtic ceremonies. It is likely that apples became associated with the holiday at this time. The Anglo-Saxons replaced the Romans as rulers of England in the fifth to seventh centuries, during which time Christianity spread throughout the land, with some of its rites being combined with existing customs. In the ninth century the Church established November 1 as All Saints' Day. The traditions of October 31 were incorporated as part of this holy day, being celebrated as the Eve of All Hallows (hallow is the Old English word for a holy person or saint), the name eventually being contracted to Halloween. The feast of All Souls on November 2 ceremonially remembered all the dead. Small pastries called soul cakes were eaten to mark the occasion. Poor people went "souling," asking for soul cakes in return for saying prayers for the dead. People carved lanterns out of large beets and turnips, and left candles burning in them to guide the souls of the dead to their former homes. Over a period of time all these observances became secularized and celebrated on Halloween.

These traditions were adapted by people from the Celtic lands when they settled in America. "Souling" became "trick or treat," with children wearing costumes representing supernatural spirits, such as ghosts and witches. The pumpkin replaced beets and turnips as a more suitable lantern to guide the spirits. The eerie orange light it emitted led to its being called "jack-o'-lantern," the colloquial English name for the mysterious flame-like phosphorescence that flits over marshy ground when the gases of decaying vegetation spontaneously ignite.

Thanksgiving The traditional Thanksgiving Day meal usually includes turkey, potatoes, corn, cranberries, and of course pumpkin pie. In this we can see a combination of the harvest festival, observed for thousands of years in many lands, and the new foods the English colonists encountered in America. We trace Thanksgiving Day back to the colony founded at Plymouth in 1620. About half the colonists died from cold and starvation that first winter, so when a good harvest was forecast the following year, Governor William Bradford declared a harvest festival to give thanks to God. The festival was held in succeeding years and spread to other colonies. Abraham Lincoln established Thanksgiving as a national holiday in November 1863. For the next 75 years Americans celebrated Thanksgiving Day on the last Thursday in November. Then President Franklin D. Roosevelt moved its observance to the fourth Thursday in the month, a move which was endorsed by Congress, who declared it a federal holiday in 1941. We have come a long way since the colonists' first harvest festival, but in our observance of this holiday we celebrate their achievement and give thanks for the bounty of our land and for the well-being of all of our loved ones.

Celebrations

Carving pumpkins The familiar face with triangular holes for eyes and nose, and a single, off-center top and bottom tooth punctuating a crescent-shaped grin is still one of the most popular for jack-o'-lanterns. Maybe this year you would like to try a ghost face, with vertical oval eyes and mouth; a cat's face with slanted oval eyes, an inverted triangular nose and whiskers made from wire or broom fibers; or even a monster with trapezoid eyes and fangs. Whether you want to maintain tradition or make your Halloween pumpkin a symbol of the times, there are some simple steps to ensure success.

First, wash the pumpkin with warm, soapy water, and dry with paper towels or a dish towel. Stand the pumpkin on newspapers spread out on your work surface. Draw a circle around the stem to serve as a guide for cutting out the lid. Insert a long-bladed, sharp knife into the line with the tip pointed at an angle towards the center. It is important to keep the knife at an angle so that the lid will be wider at the top than at the bottom to prevent it from falling into the pumpkin. Cut along the line, removing and reinserting the blade at regular intervals as you work your way around. When you have completed the circle, pull out the lid by the stem and slice off the bottom to remove the stringy fibers and seeds.

Use a sturdy, long-handled metal spoon, such as a slotted spoon, to loosen and remove the strings and seeds from inside the pumpkin. Reserve the seeds for making tasty Spiced Seeds (see page 56) to nibble. If you are planning to carve a face with curved lines or lots of detail, thin the wall from the inside by cutting or scraping away some of the pumpkin flesh, which can then be used in one of the recipes in this book.

Examine your pumpkin carefully before you begin to carve it. Choose an area free from any irregularities on which to create the face. You can draw the face you want to carve straight onto the pumpkin, but then it is not easy to alter any features, and you may be left with

For an interesting change, why not carve your jack-o'-lantern into a ghost face; a cat's face; a monster or try decorating the pumpkin with star shapes.

unwanted pen or pencil lines. It is easier to draw your design on a piece of paper first. Make sure the paper is the appropriate size and shape for the pumpkin. Draw facial features to accentuate the shape of your pumpkin. Remember that you will be cutting on a convex, ridged surface: angular lines are not difficult to cut well, but complicated wavy lines take practice to perfect. Consider also including features that can be highlighted on the surface.

Tape your drawing securely to the pumpkin so that it cannot move. Pleat the paper between the features to get it to lie flat. Use a clean, sharp, pointed implement to poke holes through the paper into the pumpkin along the lines you have drawn. Make the holes deep enough to be easily seen when you remove the paper, and close enough together to produce a clear dotted cutting line.

Place the pumpkin so that the cutting pattern is staring up at you. Using a sharp paring knife, score a line connecting the dots of each feature. Keep the knife perpendicular to the pumpkin and moving away from your body at all times. Go over the score lines with the knife several times to make a deep groove that will prevent the knife from slipping when you are cutting out.

Cut out the smaller features first. Although it may seem simpler to cut out the larger ones first, this will weaken the pumpkin shell, which might then crack or split while you are working on the others. Insert the knife in the groove in the center of the line and cut through the pumpkin wall, working away from your body toward the outer edge of the feature. Stop cutting and remove the knife before you come to the end of the line or a corner. Turning the blade to face the cut you have just made, insert it at the end of the line and work back to complete the cut. When you have cut all the way around the feature, push it in and remove it.

To produce highlights around the eyeball or cheeks, cut away the peel within the outlined area, exposing the pumpkin flesh. For finer detail, expose the flesh by scoring lines while holding the knife at an angle. To use cut-out pieces as three-dimensional features, such as ears or eyebrows, unbend a wire paper clip, insert one end halfway into the cut-out shape and the other end into the pumpkin. Place a short, fat, flat-bottomed candle in the center of the pumpkin; if you use a thinner candle, place it in the center of crumpled foil and anchor to the base of the pumpkin with straight pins. Light the candle and replace the lid. Your jack-o'-lantern is complete!

Thanksgiving decorations You can decorate the table by arranging pumpkins, gourds, pine cones, fall leaves and berries around candlesticks, or carve out scattered stars or triangles or alternating rows of slots in a pumpkin shell to create an original radiant centerpiece.

PUMPKIN AND BACON SOUP

**2 lb pumpkin, peeled, seeded
and cut into 1-inch chunks
1 onion, chopped
1 ½ cups peeled, diced carrots
1 celery stalk, trimmed and chopped
1 tablespoon soybean or sunflower oil
2 teaspoons curry powder
1 tablespoon whole-wheat flour
4 cups chicken stock
½ lb bacon, trimmed of fat and diced
salt
freshly ground black pepper**

**To Garnish:
pumpkin seeds
grated nutmeg**

1 Combine the pumpkin, onion, carrots and celery in a large saucepan with the oil. Stir-fry over a moderate heat for about 5 minutes until lightly coloured, then stir in the curry powder and cook for 1 minute more. Stir in the flour. Remove the pot from the heat and stir in the stock. Purée the pumpkin mixture in a blender or food processor, then return the purée to the pot.
2 Fry the bacon without added fat, for 3–4 minutes, stirring constantly. Drain off any fat and add the bacon to the soup. Taste, and adjust the seasoning if necessary, then bring the soup to a boil. Simmer for 5 minutes, stirring.
3 Serve the soup in warm bowls, garnished with pumpkin seeds and grated nutmeg.

Serves 6
Preparation time: 15 minutes
Cooking time: 20 minutes

GINGERED PUMPKIN SOUP

2 ¼ lb pumpkin, peeled, seeded
and roughly chopped
1 1-inch piece fresh ginger, peeled
1 tablespoon sunflower oil
1 large onion, peeled and chopped
2 teaspoons ground ginger
1 teaspoon ground turmeric
2 ripe tomatoes, skinned and chopped
2 teaspoons light brown sugar
¼ teaspoon grated nutmeg
1 strip thinly pared orange zest
2 ½ cups chicken stock
salt
freshly ground black pepper
1 ¼ cups plain yogurt

To Garnish:
2 tablespoons chopped parsley
6 tablespoons pumpkin seeds

1 Put the pumpkin and the piece of ginger into a saucepan and cover with water. Bring to a boil, cover the pot and simmer for 15 minutes or until the pumpkin is tender. Drain thoroughly and discard the piece of ginger.
2 Heat the oil in a clean saucepan, add the onion and fry over moderate heat for 2 minutes. Stir in the ground ginger and turmeric, and cook for 1 minute.
3 Add the pumpkin, tomatoes, sugar, nutmeg, orange zest and stock, and bring to a boil. Cover and simmer for 10 minutes. Cool slightly. Discard the orange zest.
4 Purée the pumpkin mixture in a blender or food processor, then return the purée to the pot. Season to taste with salt and pepper, and stir in the yogurt. Heat gently. Taste, and adjust the seasoning if necessary.
5 Serve in warm bowls, garnished with the parsley and pumpkin seeds.

Serves 6
Preparation time: 15 minutes
Cooking time: 40 minutes

PUMPKIN AND LEMON SOUP

¼ cup butter
1 large onion, sliced
1 lb pumpkin, peeled, seeded and
cut into chunks
1 ¾ cups sliced potatoes
1 small garlic clove, crushed
a sprig of fresh thyme
5 cups chicken stock
salt
freshly ground black pepper
2 tablespoons lemon juice
⅔ cup heavy cream

1 Melt the butter in a large heavy saucepan and slowly cook the onion until soft and transparent. Add the pumpkin, potatoes, garlic and thyme, cover the pot and simmer for 20 minutes or until all the vegetables are soft.
2 Add the stock, and salt and pepper to taste. Bring to a boil, and simmer for 10 minutes. Remove and discard the thyme sprig.
3 Purée the soup in a blender or food processor. Stir in the lemon juice and then the cream. Return to the pot and reheat, but do not boil. Serve in warm bowls.

Serves 6
Preparation time: 30 minutes
Cooking time: 50 minutes

PUMPKIN SOUP

For an impressive serving idea, serve the soup in the hollowed out pumpkin shell, see page 10 for instructions.

¼ cup butter or margarine
2 lb pumpkin, peeled, seeded and cut into large pieces
⅔ cup warm water
a pinch of grated nutmeg
a pinch of dried thyme
salt
white pepper
6 ¼ cups milk
¼ cup long-grain white rice

Croutons:
3 slices white bread, crusts removed
1 tablespoon sunflower oil
2 tablespoons butter

1 Melt the butter or margarine in a large saucepan. Add the pumpkin, stir well and cook over low to moderate heat for 10 minutes. Add the water, nutmeg and thyme, and salt and pepper to taste. Cover and cook over a high heat until the pumpkin is soft.

2 Purée the pumpkin mixture in a blender or food processor until smooth, adding a little of the milk if necessary. Return the purée to a clean saucepan.

3 Add the remaining milk and rice to the pumpkin purée, stir well, cover and cook for 30 minutes or until the rice is tender, stirring occasionally.

4 Meanwhile, make the croutons. Cut the bread into small cubes. Heat the oil and butter together in a frying pan, add the bread and fry until golden brown on all sides, stirring frequently. Drain on paper towels.

5 Serve in warm bowls with the croutons sprinkled on top.

Serves 6
Preparation time: 10 minutes
Cooking time: 40–45 minutes

HEARTY PUMPKIN SOUP

1 ½ lb pumpkin, peeled, seeded and diced
1 onion, chopped
¼ cup brown rice
1 lb carrots, sliced lengthwise
5 cups boiling chicken stock
¼ teaspoon ground nutmeg
4-inch stick of cinnamon, halved
¼ teaspoon ground mixed spice
salt
freshly ground black pepper
1 cup frozen peas
1 orange, to garnish

1 Place the pumpkin, onion, rice, carrots and stock in a large saucepan. Add the spices, and salt and pepper to taste, and simmer for about 45 minutes until the rice is soft. Add the peas and cook for 5 minutes more. Remove and discard the cinnamon stick.

2 Cut 4 thin slices from the center of the orange for the garnish. Grate the rest of the zest and squeeze out the juice. Stir the grated zest and the juice into the soup.

3 Serve in heated bowls, each garnished with a twisted orange slice.

Serves 4
Preparation time: 10 minutes
Cooking time: 50 minutes

FRIED PUMPKIN

1 lb pumpkin, peeled, seeded and sliced
salt
freshly ground pepper
2 tablespoons all-purpose flour
1 egg, beaten
2 tablespoons dried bread crumbs
oil for frying

1 Sprinkle the pumpkin slices with salt and pepper. Dip them in the flour, then in the egg and finally in the bread crumbs.
2 Heat the oil in a frying pan. When it is hot, add the pumpkin slices and fry until golden brown on both sides.
3 Drain on paper towels and serve immediately.

Serves 3–4
Preparation time: 5 minutes
Cooking time: 15 minutes

NAVY BEANS WITH PUMPKIN AND CORN

Tomatoes, beans, corn and pumpkin all originated in Mexico and gradually spread throughout Central and South America. This particular combination is from Chile.

1 cup dried navy beans
2 tablespoons sweet paprika
¼ cup olive oil
2 onions, finely chopped
1 lb pumpkin, peeled, seeded and cut into 1-inch cubes
2 green chilies, seeded and chopped
kernels from 2 large ears of fresh corn or
1 cup frozen or canned corn kernels
1 lb tomatoes, blanched, skinned and chopped
½ teaspoon dried oregano
salt
freshly ground black pepper

1 Soak the beans in cold water for 3–4 hours. Place in unsalted water in a saucepan, bring to a slow boil, reduce the heat and simmer for 1 ½–2 hours, or until tender. Set aside.
2 Mix the paprika with the oil in a heavy, deep frying pan over a moderate heat. Add the onions and fry until they are tender. Add the pumpkin, chilies, corn, tomatoes, oregano, salt and pepper, and simmer for 5 minutes.
3 Drain the beans, reserving the liquid. Add the beans to the tomato mixture, adding a little of the cooking liquid if the purée is very dry. Cover the pan and simmer gently for 15 minutes to blend the flavors. The pumpkin will disintegrate and thicken the sauce. Serve in warm soup bowls.

Serves 6
Preparation time: 20 minutes plus soaking and simmering time
Cooking time: 25 minutes

SWEET AND SOUR PUMPKIN

A delightful blend of flavors, this dish comes from Sicily, where it is called zucca all'agrodolce.

vegetable oil for frying
1 ¼ lb pumpkin, peeled,
seeded and thinly sliced
3–4 tablespoons wine vinegar
2 tablespoons sugar
1 tablespoon fresh chopped mint
2 garlic cloves, crushed
salt
freshly ground black pepper

1 Pour the oil to a depth of ¼ inch into a large frying pan and place over the heat. When the oil is hot, add the pumpkin slices and fry until golden brown on both sides.

2 Drain off most of the oil from the pan, then add the vinegar, sugar, mint, garlic, and salt and pepper to taste. Cook for 10 minutes more, turning the pumpkin slices over halfway through the cooking. Serve immediately.

Serves 4
Preparation time: 5 minutes
Cooking time: 25 minutes

CREAM-GLAZED PUMPKIN

4 slices bacon
1 tablespoon butter
2 lb pumpkin, peeled, seeded and
cut into ½-inch cubes
¼ cup water
¼ cup heavy cream
½ teaspoon ground cinnamon
salt
freshly ground black pepper
coarsely chopped pecans,
to garnish (optional)

1 Cook the bacon in a wide frying pan until crisp and the fat is rendered. Remove the bacon and drain on paper towels. When it is cool enough to handle, crumble the bacon coarsely.

2 Pour off all but 1 tablespoon of the bacon fat from the frying pan. Add the butter and melt it, then add the pumpkin cubes and water. Stir to mix, cover, and steam over a moderate heat for 15–20 minutes or until the pumpkin is just tender. Do not over-cook. Stir occasionally to prevent sticking.

3 Stir in the cream, cinnamon, and salt and pepper to taste. Cook uncovered, stirring, until the pumpkin is glazed and almost all the liquid has been absorbed. Spoon into a hot serving dish and sprinkle the bacon and pecans, if using, over the top.

Serves 4
Preparation time: 10 minutes
Cooking time: 40–45 minutes

BAKED PUMPKIN

One of the simplest dishes to prepare, baked pumpkin can be served as a vegetable dish with a main course or as a light lunch with a mixed salad.

2–2 ½ lb pumpkin, divided into quarters or wedges and seeded
1 tablespoon butter
salt
freshly ground black pepper

1 Preheat the oven to 375°F.

2 Dot the pumpkin sections with butter, and season with salt and pepper. Place on a greased baking sheet and bake for about 50 minutes. Baste with butter occasionally until the pumpkin is tender. Serve immediately.

Serves 4
Preparation time: 3 minutes
Cooking time: about 50 minutes

PUMPKIN SALAD

2 small pumpkins, washed
4 garlic cloves
salt
2 tablespoons butter, melted
lemon juice

Filling:
I cup long-grain white rice, cooked
2 cups peas, cooked
2 ¼ cups shredded white
cabbage, blanched
I red bell pepper, cored,
seeded and chopped
I fennel bulb chopped
I Jerusalem artichoke, washed,
scraped and shredded
4 ripe tomatoes, skinned,
seeded and chopped
⅓ cup golden raisins
I small apple, shredded
I tablespoon chopped parsley
I teaspoon caraway seeds
2 tablespoons wine vinegar
I tablespoon olive oil
coarsely ground black pepper

1 Preheat the oven to 350°F.

2 Cut off the tops of the pumpkins about a quarter of the way down. Scoop out the seeds and pulp.

3 Rub the insides of both pumpkins with a cut garlic clove and sprinkle with salt. Put 1 garlic clove in each pumpkin, replace the lids and bake for 35 minutes, then brush the insides with the butter and a little more salt, and bake for 15 minutes more.

4 Scoop out about half the flesh from each pumpkin and mash 3 tablespoons of it with the cooked garlic. Crush the remaining garlic cloves and combine with the mashed pumpkin and the remainder of scooped out flesh. Sprinkle with a little lemon juice and spread inside the pumpkins.

5 When the pumpkins are cold, place all the filling ingredients in a bowl and mix thoroughly. Spoon the mixture into the pumpkins and serve.

Serves 12
Preparation time: 40 minutes
Cooking time: 50 minutes

TWICE-BAKED STUFFED PUMPKIN

2 lb pumpkin, seeded and
cut into quarters or wedges
3 tablespoons butter
salt
freshly ground black pepper
I egg yolk, lightly beaten
I tablespoon heavy cream

Filling:
I tablespoon butter
¼ cup ground beef
¼ cup finely chopped salt pork or ham
I tomato, skinned, seeded and chopped
½ onion, finely chopped

I Preheat the oven to 375°F. Dot the pumpkin pieces with 1 tablespoon of the butter, add salt and pepper to taste, place on a greased baking sheet and bake for about 50 minutes. Baste with butter occasionally until tender.
2 Meanwhile, make the filling. Heat the butter in a frying pan, add the ground beef and salt pork or ham, and fry until thoroughly cooked. Add the tomato, onion, salt and pepper, and toss with a fork to blend well.
3 Remove the pumpkin from the oven and increase the temperature to 425°F. Scoop out the cooked pumpkin and mash well with the remaining butter, egg yolk, and season to taste. Stir in the cream and press the mixture back into the shells. Put a quarter of the filling in the center of each wedge, place on a greased baking sheet and bake for 15 minutes.

Serves 4
Preparation time: 15 minutes
Cooking time: 65 minutes

PUMPKIN CURRY

I lb pumpkin, peeled, seeded
and cut into cubes
⅛ cup tightly packed dried tamarind pods
(see note)
I cup very hot water
3 tablespoons oil
½ teaspoon cumin seeds
¼ teaspoon mustard seeds
¼ teaspoon fenugreek seeds
¼ teaspoon onion seeds
¼ teaspoon aniseed
3 potatoes, peeled and cut into chunks
I teaspoon chili powder
½ teaspoon ground turmeric
I teaspoon ground coriander
I teaspoon sugar
salt

I Wash the pumpkin cubes and drain well.
2 Soak the tamarind pods in the hot water for 10–15 minutes. Remove the pods, reserving the liquid, and extract the pulp by mashing in a bowl with the back of a spoon. Strain to remove seeds and string.
3 Heat the oil in a frying pan, add the cumin seeds, mustard seeds, fenugreek, onion seeds and aniseed, and fry for 30 seconds. Add the potato chunks and fry for 2–3 minutes. Add the pumpkin cubes, stir well and fry for 4–5 minutes.
4 Stir in the chili powder, turmeric, coriander, sugar, and salt to taste, and continue frying for 5–6 minutes. Add the tamarind pulp and some of the reserved liquid, to taste, then cover and cook until the potatoes are tender. Note: If dried tamarind pods are not available, substitute 1 tablespoon molasses and 3 tablespoons lime juice mixed together.

Serves 4
Preparation time: 25 minutes
Cooking time: 30 minutes

PUMPKIN-FILLED RAVIOLI

Pasta:
4 cups all-purpose flour
3 eggs
I teaspoon olive oil
3–4 tablespoons water

Filling:
2 lb pumpkin, seeded
2 eggs
¼ cup grated Parmesan cheese
I cup crushed Amaretti cookies
or macaroons
2 ½ cups fresh bread crumbs
¼ cup finely chopped sweet chutney
salt
¼ teaspoon grated nutmeg

I To prepare the pasta, put the flour in a bowl. Make a well in the center of the flour and drop in the eggs. Add the oil and draw the flour into the center using your hand. Gradually add the water, 1 tablespoon at a time. You may not need to add all the water, depending on how absorbent the flour is. Knead to a firm dough (firmer than a pastry or bread dough).

2 Continue kneading, folding the dough over and over and working it with the heel of your hand, until it is smooth. Cover in plastic wrap and let it rest for a minimum of 15 minutes and a maximum of 2 hours before rolling.

3 Meanwhile, prepare the filling. Place the pumpkin with the peel on in a large saucepan of salted water and bring to the boil for about 30 minutes or until tender. Quarter the cooked pieces and leave to cool at room temperature. Remove the peel, place the pumpkin flesh in a clean muslin cloth, tie the cloth in a knot and let it drain for 2 hours. Squeeze after draining.

4 Pass the pumpkin through a strainer into a bowl. Add the eggs, Parmesan, cookies, bread crumbs, chutney, salt and nutmeg, and mix.

5 Roll out the dough on a lightly floured surface with a long floured rolling pin to make 2 large rectangles. Roll out the dough as thinly as possible without tearing it (you should be able to see through the pasta). Arrange the pumpkin mixture in tiny portions about the size of a hazelnut and at equal intervals on top of 1 sheet of pasta. Brush around the edges of the pasta with a slightly dampened pastry brush and lay the second sheet of pasta on top. Press down around each knob with your fingers to seal, and cut out the squares with a crimped pastry wheel. Seal the edges with a fork. Let dry at room temperature for 1 hour.

6 To cook, drop the ravioli into a deep saucepan of salted boiling water and cook for 6-8 minutes, depending on size, stirring occasionally. Drain thoroughly and serve immediately.

Serves 4–6
Preparation time: 50 minutes plus resting, draining and drying time
Cooking time: about 40 minutes

PUMPKIN, CHICKPEA AND BANANA CURRY

Although this combination of flavors might sound unusual, it produces a really tasty dish to serve with plain or spiced rice.

3 tablespoons sunflower oil
1 small onion, sliced
2 garlic cloves, chopped
2 teaspoons grated fresh ginger
1 teaspoon ground coriander
½ teaspoon ground cumin
½ teaspoon ground turmeric
¼ teaspoon ground cinnamon
1 ¼ lb pumpkin, peeled, seeded and cut into cubes
2 tablespoons hot curry paste
2 ripe tomatoes, chopped
2 dried red chilies
1 ¼ cups vegetable stock
1 ¾ cups canned chickpeas, drained
1 large underripe banana
1 tablespoon chopped fresh cilantro

1 Heat 2 tablespoons of the oil in a saucepan, add the onion, garlic, ginger and ground spices, and fry over a medium heat for about 5–6 minutes until the onion is lightly browned.

2 Place the pumpkin in a bowl, add the curry paste and toss well to coat the pumpkin evenly.

3 Add the tomatoes, chilies and stock to the onion mixture, bring to a boil and simmer gently for 15 minutes.

4 Meanwhile, heat the remaining oil in a nonstick frying pan, add the coated pumpkin and fry for 5 minutes until golden. Add to the tomato sauce with the chickpeas, cover and cook for 20 minutes until the pumpkin is tender.

5 Peel the banana, slice thickly and stir into the curry 5 minutes before the end of the cooking time. Stir in the chopped cilantro and serve immediately.

Serves 4
Preparation time: 25 minutes
Cooking time: 50 minutes

STUFFED PUMPKIN

2 lb pumpkin
I tablespoon butter
I onion, finely chopped
½ cup ground beef
salt
freshly ground black pepper
¼ cup crisp dried bread crumbs
¼ cup shredded Cheddar cheese

1 Preheat the oven to 400°F.
2 Cook the pumpkin in boiling water for about 20 minutes, until it becomes a little soft.
3 Meanwhile, heat the butter in a frying pan, add the onion and cook until transparent. Add the meat, mix well and season to taste with salt and pepper. Simmer over a low heat for about 15 minutes or until the meat is cooked through.
4 Cut the pumpkin into quarters, scoop out and discard the seeds and fibers. Scoop out the flesh, keeping the shells intact. Chop and mash the half-cooked pumpkin flesh, and add to the meat, with more salt and pepper if required, and simmer for 2 minutes.
5 Pile the filling back into the shells, and sprinkle the bread crumbs and shredded cheese on top. Place on a greased baking sheet and bake for about 20 minutes until delicately browned.

Serves 4
Preparation time: 10 minutes
Cooking time: 50 minutes

PUMPKIN OMELET

I ½ cups diced pumpkin
¼ cup butter or margarine
2 canned red bell peppers, diced
6–8 eggs
2 tablespoons light cream or milk
salt
I tablespoon chopped chives
I tablespoon chopped parsley
I teaspoon grated lemon zest

1 Preheat the oven to 425°F.
2 Steam the diced pumpkin until tender.
3 Put the butter or margarine in an 8–9-inch round ovenproof dish and place toward the top of the oven until melted. Add the pumpkin and peppers, and replace in the oven for another 4 minutes.
4 Beat the eggs with the remaining ingredients, pour over the pumpkin and pepper mixture and replace in the oven just above the middle.
5 Bake for 10–15 minutes or until set to taste.

Serves 4
Preparation time: 15 minutes
Cooking time: 20–25 minutes

STIR-FRIED PUMPKIN WITH LAMB

2 garlic cloves
¼-inch piece fresh ginger, finely chopped
2 teaspoons coriander seeds, toasted
1 tablespoon grated lemon zest
3 tablespoons lemon juice
1 1-inch piece green chili, seeded and finely sliced
1 lb lean lamb from leg, cut into thin strips
2 ½ tablespoons olive oil
1 ¾ lb pumpkin, peeled, seeded and cut into ¾-inch cubes
½ cup vegetable stock
2 tablespoons chopped cilantro
salt
freshly ground black pepper

1 Place the garlic, ginger, 1 teaspoon of the coriander seeds, the lemon zest, lemon juice and half the chili in a mortar and grind to make a paste. Place the lamb in a bowl and mix in the paste. Cover and refrigerate for 4–6 hours.

2 Heat 2 tablespoons of the oil in a large frying pan. Add the pumpkin and remaining coriander seeds and chili. Stir-fry over a medium heat until evenly brown. Add a little vegetable stock. Cover the pan and cook over a low heat for 2 minutes. Set aside and keep warm.

3 Heat the remaining oil in a wok. Add the lamb and marinade, and stir-fry over a high heat for 4–5 minutes until evenly browned. Add the pumpkin mixture and stir-fry until heated through, adding more stock if necessary. Stir in the cilantro, add salt and pepper to taste, and serve.

Serves 4–6
Preparation time: 15 minutes plus refrigeration time
Cooking time: 15 minutes

PUMPKIN AND SAGE RISOTTO WITH PINE NUT SAUCE

This is a rich and creamy risotto, with the slightly unusual inclusion of a pine nut sauce. When pumpkin is not available use 2 cups winter squash instead and substitute rosemary for the sage.

2 tablespoons extra virgin olive oil
1 large onion, finely chopped
1 garlic clove, minced
1–2 tablespoons fresh sage
1 ½ cups aborio rice
2 cups pumpkin flesh, diced
3 ½ cups boiling vegetable stock
⅓ cup pine nuts
⅓ cup freshly shredded Parmesan cheese
4 tablespoons milk
pinch of ground nutmeg
salt and pepper

1 Heat the oil in a large pan and sauté the onion, garlic, and sage for about 5 minutes until golden. Add the rice and pumpkin and stir-fry for 1 minute until all the rice grains are well coated in oil.
2 Add ¼ pint of stock and simmer, stirring until absorbed. Continue to add the stock a little at a time, stirring frequently, for about 25 minutes, until the rice is creamy and all the liquid is absorbed.
3 Meanwhile, process the pine nuts, cheese, milk, and nutmeg in a blender until smooth. Stir into the risotto, with the final addition of stock, and simmer for a further 5 minutes. Season to taste and serve at once.

Serves 4
Preparation time: 20 minutes
Cooking time: 35–40 minutes

BRAISED PORK WITH PUMPKIN

4 tablespoons soy sauce
3 tablespoons dry sherry
¾ lb lean pork roast, cut into ½-inch slices
2 tablespoons oil
1 lb pumpkin, peeled, seeded and cut into 1-inch cubes
4 green onions, each cut into 3 pieces
1 piece fresh ginger, shredded
2 garlic cloves, sliced

To Garnish:
carrots cut into flower shapes
sliced green onions
cilantro leaves

1 Put the soy sauce and sherry in a bowl, stir, add the pork, mix well, and marinate for 20 minutes.
2 Heat the oil in a wok or frying pan, add the pumpkin and fry quickly until browned. Add the green onions, ginger and garlic, and cook for 1 minute. Add the pork and marinade, and cook for 12–15 minutes, until the pork and pumpkin are tender.
3 Spoon the pork mixture onto a warm serving dish, garnish with carrot flowers, green onion slices and cilantro leaves, and serve immediately.

Serves 4–6
Preparation time: 30 minutes
Cooking time: 20 minutes

PUMPKIN PASTA

1 lb pumpkin, peeled, seeded and
cut into large chunks
4 cups all-purpose flour
2 large eggs
1 teaspoon olive oil
3–4 tablespoons water
salt

To Garnish:
butter
chopped parsley

1 Steam or boil the pumpkin for 20–30 minutes until tender. Purée in a blender or food processor. If the purée seems too wet, put it in a saucepan and dry it over a low heat for 1–2 minutes, stirring occasionally with a wooden spoon.

2 Put the purée into a large bowl and add the flour gradually, stirring and keeping the mixture smooth. Make a well in the center and drop in the eggs. Add the oil and draw the flour and pumpkin mixture into the center with your hand. Add the water, 1 tablespoon at a time. You may not need to add all the water, depending on how absorbent the flour is. Knead to a firm dough.

3 Continue kneading, folding the dough over and over and working it with the heel of your hand, until it is smooth. Cover in plastic wrap and let it rest for about 30 minutes before rolling.

4 Roll out the dough on a lightly floured surface with a long, floured rolling pin. Roll out the dough as thinly as possible without tearing it (you should be able to see through the pasta). To turn the dough, roll it lightly over the rolling pin.

5 Let the pasta dry on a clean dish towel for about 10 minutes, then roll it into a scroll and cut it in strips to your preferred width. Bring a deep pot of water to a boil, add salt, then drop in the pasta and cook for about 4 minutes, stirring occasionally.

6 Drain in a colander, but do not rinse. Pour into a serving bowl, mix with butter, sprinkle with chopped parsley and serve.

Makes 1 lb
Preparation time: 30 minutes plus resting time
Cooking time: 40 minutes

SPICY PUMPKIN CASSEROLE

Serve this South American casserole in the cooking dish, with a seasonal salad.

2 ¼ cups water
2 tablespoons lemon juice
salt
2 lb pumpkin, peeled, seeded and cut into chunks
3 cups cooked long-grain white rice
½ lb garlic sausage, skinned and sliced
2–3 tablespoons fresh bread crumbs, moistened in a little milk
1 cup shredded Swiss cheese
1 tablespoon butter

Béchamel Sauce:
2 tablespoons butter or margarine
2 tablespoons all-purpose flour
1 ¼ cups milk, warmed
freshly ground black pepper

1 Preheat the oven to 425°F.
2 Put the water, lemon juice and a pinch of salt in a large saucepan and bring to a boil. Add the pumpkin, bring back to a boil, lower the heat and cook gently for about 40 minutes or until tender.
3 Meanwhile, prepare the béchamel sauce. Melt the butter or margarine in a small saucepan, add the flour and cook for 2–3 minutes. Gradually whisk in the milk. Bring to a boil, stirring constantly. Lower the heat and simmer gently for about 10 minutes, then season with salt and pepper to taste.
4 Drain the pumpkin thoroughly. Arrange in alternate layers with the rice and sausage in an ovenproof dish, spooning a little of the béchamel sauce over each layer. Sprinkle the bread crumbs and cheese over the top, and dot with butter. Cook in the oven for about 15 minutes or until the top is golden brown and crisp.

Serves 4

Preparation time: 15 minutes
Cooking time: 1 ¼ hours

PUMPKIN, ONION AND TOMATO GRATIN

1 tablespoon butter
1 large onion
1 garlic clove, crushed
1 lb pumpkin, peeled, seeded and cut into 1-inch slices
2 cups canned tomatoes with their juices
1 teaspoon dried basil
1 teaspoon dried oregano
salt
freshly ground black pepper
¾ cup shredded Cheddar cheese
¼ cup shredded Gruyère cheese
1 ½ cups fresh whole-wheat bread crumbs

1 Melt the butter in a deep frying pan. Add the onion and garlic, and fry until soft. Add the pumpkin, tomatoes with their juices, basil, oregano, and salt and pepper to taste. Bring to a boil, cover and simmer for 30–35 minutes or until the pumpkin is soft. Pour into a shallow heatproof dish. Preheat the broiler.
2 Mix together the cheeses and bread crumbs. Sprinkle over the vegetables and place the dish under the broiler for 2–3 minutes until the top is golden brown. Serve immediately.

Serves 4

Preparation time: 15 minutes
Cooking time: 40–45 minutes

PUMPKIN GRIDDLE CAKES

Corn and pumpkin were staples in the diets of Native Americans and the early settlers, so these griddle cakes have a long tradition.

1 cup fine yellow cornmeal
1 tablespoon light brown sugar
½ teaspoon salt
½ teaspoon baking soda
½ cup Pumpkin Purée (see page 31)
⅓ cup water
1 large egg, beaten
2 tablespoons browned butter or melted bacon fat
butter or bacon fat for frying
maple syrup, to serve (optional)

1 Mix the cornmeal, sugar, salt and baking soda in a large bowl. Add the pumpkin purée, water and egg, and mix well. Stir in the melted butter or bacon fat.
2 Grease a stove-top griddle or heavy frying pan and heat until very hot. Drop heaping tablespoons of batter onto the griddle or pan and fry until lightly browned, turning once. Serve with maple syrup, if liked.

Makes about 12
Preparation time: 10 minutes
Cooking time: 25 minutes

WINTER NUT GRATIN

1 cup roughly chopped carrots
2 parsnips, diced
2 lb pumpkin, peeled, seeded and diced
1 leek sliced
⅔ cup milk
1 ¼ cups vegetable stock
1 ½ cups canned chestnuts, drained
salt
freshly ground black pepper
2 tablespoons cornstarch blended with
1 tablespoon water
2 tablespoons sunflower seeds
¼ cup chopped nuts
1 cup fresh whole-wheat bread crumbs
½ cup shredded Cheddar cheese
fresh herbs, to garnish

1 Place the carrots, parsnips, pumpkin and leek in a large saucepan with the milk and stock, and bring to a boil. Partly cover and simmer for 15–20 minutes until almost tender. Add the chestnuts, salt and pepper to taste, and stir well.
2 Stir in the blended cornstarch and cook until thickened, stirring constantly.
3 Preheat the broiler.
4 Transfer the mixture to a warm ovenproof dish. Mix together the sunflower seeds, nuts, bread crumbs and cheese, and sprinkle evenly over the top. Place under the broiler for about 5 minutes until the top is crisp and golden brown. Serve immediately, garnished with fresh herbs.

Serves 4
Preparation time: 40 minutes
Cooking time: 30 minutes

VEGETABLE GOULASH

2 tablespoons vegetable oil
I large onion
I tablespoon paprika
2 ⅓ cups canned tomatoes with their juices
I large green bell pepper, cored,
seeded and chopped
I ¼ cups sliced carrots
2 cups diced potatoes
I ¼ cups diced pumpkin
⅔ cup sour cream
salt and pepper

1 Preheat the oven to 350°F.

2 Heat the oil in a flameproof casserole, add the onion and cook until soft. Add the paprika and cook for 1 minute. Add the tomatoes and their juices, then bring to a boil.

3 Add the green pepper, carrots, potatoes and pumpkin to the casserole, and season to taste with salt and pepper. Cover, and cook in the oven for 1–1 ¼ hours, stirring occasionally.

4 Remove the casserole from the oven and put on the stove over a low heat. Stir in most of the sour cream and reheat gently without boiling. Put the remaining sour cream on top of the casserole immediately before serving.

Serves 4
Preparation time: 20 minutes
Cooking time: 1 ¼–1 ½ hours

WINTER STEW

2–3 tablespoons vegetable oil

1 large onion, chopped

1 lb pumpkin, peeled, seeded and cut into bite-sized pieces

2 leeks, halved lengthwise, washed and sliced

3 potatoes, peeled, cut in chunks

1 tablespoon all-purpose flour

5 cups hot vegetable stock

1 tablespoon tomato paste

¼ teaspoon celery seeds

salt

freshly ground black pepper

1 tablespoon chopped parsley, to garnish

Dumplings:

2 tablespoons butter or margarine

1 cup self-rising whole-wheat flour

1 teaspoon dried mixed herbs

1 tablespoon vegetable oil

8 tablespoons water

1 Preheat the oven to 400°F.

2 Reserve 1 tablespoon of the oil. Heat a little of the remaining oil in a saucepan, and fry the onion quickly until golden brown. Transfer to an ovenproof casserole.

3 Add a little more oil to the pan as necessary and brown the pumpkin, leeks and potatoes in batches, then transfer to the casserole with the onion.

4 Add the reserved tablespoon of oil to the pan, stir in the flour, and cook over a steady heat, stirring, until the flour is browned. Gradually pour in the stock and bring to a boil and cook, stirring, until the sauce has thickened. Add the tomato paste, celery seeds, and salt and pepper, then pour over the vegetables in the casserole. Cover and cook in the oven for 50 minutes.

5 Meanwhile, make the dumplings. Rub the butter or margarine into the flour until the mixture resembles bread crumbs. Add the dried herbs, salt and pepper to taste, oil and water. Mix to a soft dough and shape into 8 balls.

6 When the casserole has cooked for 50 minutes, remove the lid and add the dumplings. Replace the lid and return the casserole to the oven for 20–30 minutes more. The dumplings will rise to the top and double in size. Serve the winter stew hot, garnished with chopped parsley.

Serves 4

Preparation time: 30 minutes

Cooking time: 1 ½ hours

PUMPKIN PIE I

2 x Shortcrust Pastry (see below)
1 cup Pumpkin Purée (see below)
2 eggs, beaten
⅔ cup light cream
½ cup firmly packed dark brown sugar
1 teaspoon ground cinnamon
½ teaspoon ground ginger
¼ teaspoon grated nutmeg

To Decorate:
⅔ cup confectioner's sugar
ground cinnamon

1 Preheat the oven to 375°F.
2 Roll out half the pastry on a lightly floured surface and use to line a 9-inch pie plate. Roll out the other half thinly and cut into leaf shapes. Brush the edge of the pastry lightly with water and attach the leaves.
3 Mix the pumpkin purée, eggs, light cream, sugar and spices in a large bowl. Pour into the pastry case. Use pastry trimmimgs to cut acorn and leaf shapes to decorate the pie. Bake for 45–50 minutes, until the filling has set. Set aside to cool.

Serves 6–8
Preparation time: 25 minutes
Cooking time: 45–50 minutes

SHORTCRUST PASTRY

1 cup all-purpose flour
½ cup chilled butter, diced
2 tablespoons sugar
3–4 tablespoons cold water

1 Place the flour in a bowl, add the butter and rub in with your fingertips until the mixture resembles fine bread crumbs. Stir in the sugar, then add enough of the cold water to mix to a firm dough. Knead briefly.

Makes enough dough to line an 8–9-inch pie plate
Preparation time: 10 minutes

PUMPKIN PURÉE

Use this simple recipe to make purée for all your pumpkin desserts. You can substitute canned pumpkin purée, but make sure it does not have any added sugar.

1 lb pumpkin, peeled, seeded and cut into chunks

1 Steam or boil the pumpkin for 15–20 minutes until tender, then drain thoroughly. Purée in a blender or food processor, and strain.

Makes 1 cup
Preparation time: 5 minutes
Cooking time: 15–20 minutes

PUMPKIN PIE II

Pastry:
1 cup all-purpose flour
a pinch of salt
¼ cup lard
¼ cup butter or margarine, diced
2 tablespoons cold water
whipped cream, to serve

Filling:
1 ¾ cups Pumpkin Purée (see page 34)
¾ cup sugar
1 tablespoon cornstarch
1 tablespoon light molasses
2 teaspoons mixed spice
⅔ cup light cream
3 eggs, well-beaten

1 To make the pastry, sift the flour and salt into a bowl, add the lard and butter or margarine, and rub in with your fingertips until the mixture resembles fine bread crumbs. Add the water and mix to a firm dough. Knead lightly. Wrap in plastic wrap and chill in the refrigerator for at least 15 minutes before using.

2 Preheat the oven to 400°F. Roll out the chilled pastry fairly thinly on a lightly floured surface and use to line a lightly greased 9-inch tart pan.

3 To make the filling, put all the ingredients into a bowl and beat with a wooden spoon until thoroughly combined. Pour the mixture into the pastry case.

4 Bake for 45 minutes, then open the oven door, turn off the heat and leave the pie in the oven for 15 minutes more. Serve warm with whipped cream.

Serves 6–8
Preparation time: 20 minutes
Cooking time: 45 minutes, plus 15 minutes resting

RUM PUMPKIN PIE

1 x Shortcrust Pastry (see page 34)
3 eggs
2 cups Pumpkin Purée (see page 34)
¾ cup firmly packed dark brown sugar
¼ cup dark rum
1 tablespoon black molasses
¼ teaspoon ground ginger
¼ teaspoon grated nutmeg
½ teaspoon ground cinnamon
¼ teaspoon ground cloves
¼ teaspoon salt
1 cup milk

To Decorate:
softly whipped cream
pumpkin-shaped Halloween Pumpkin
Cookies (see page 46), sprinkled
with sugar

1 Preheat the oven to 450°F.
2 Roll out the pastry on a lightly floured surface and use to line a 9-inch pie plate.
3 Beat the eggs lightly in a large bowl. Add the pumpkin purée, brown sugar, rum, molasses, spices and salt, and mix well. Stir in the milk thoroughly.
4 Pull out the middle shelf of the oven halfway. Place the pie plate on the shelf and carefully ladle in the filling: it is very liquid. Gently slide the shelf into the oven and bake for 10 minutes, then lower the heat to 350°F and bake for 35–40 minutes more, until the filling seems set, except for the very center, which should shiver slightly when the pie plate is gently moved.
5 Cool on a wire tray. Decorate with softly whipped cream and pumpkin-shaped cookies. The pie may be served warm or cold, but not hot.

Serves 6–8
Preparation time: 25 minutes
Cooking time: about 50 minutes

PUMPKIN PUDDING

1 lb pumpkin, peeled, seeded and cubed
⅔ cup apple cider
⅓ cup firmly packed light brown sugar
¼ teaspoon mixed spice
¼ cup butter
2 eggs, separated
¼ cup sugar
2 tablespoons slivered almonds

1 Preheat the oven to 375°F.

2 Put the pumpkin in cubes in a saucepan with the apple cider, brown sugar and spice. Cover the pan and simmer gently until the pumpkin is tender.

3 Beat the cooked pumpkin to a purée, then beat in the butter and egg yolks. Set aside to cool.

4 Whisk the egg whites until stiff. Whisk in the sugar. Fold the meringue lightly but thoroughly into the pumpkin mixture.

5 Spoon the pumpkin mixture into four individual greased ramekins or a greased shallow ovenproof dish. Sprinkle with the slivered almonds. Bake for 30–35 minutes. Serve hot.

Serves 4
Preparation time: 20 minutes
Cooking time: 50–55 minutes

CREAMY PUMPKIN PIE

Pastry:
3 cups whole-wheat flour
¼ teaspoon salt
¾ cup margarine
2 teaspoons sugar
2 egg yolks
cold water
I cup heavy cream, whipped, to decorate

Filling:
2 ½ cups Pumpkin Purée (see page 34)
I ¼ cup firmly packed light brown sugar
4 teaspoons ground cinnamon
2 teaspoons grated nutmeg
2 teaspoons ground ginger
4 eggs, beaten
I ¼ cups light cream
I cup fresh orange juice
4–6 tablespoons grated orange zest

I Preheat the oven to 375°F.

2 To make the pastry, sift the flour and salt into a bowl, add the margarine and rub in with your fingertips until the mixture resembles fine bread crumbs. Stir in the sugar, then add the egg yolks and enough cold water to mix to a pliable dough.

3 Turn the dough out onto a lightly floured surface and knead briefly. Roll out and use to line two 8-inch tart pans or flan dishes. Place them on a baking sheet and chill while you make the filling.

4 Put the pumpkin purée, sugar, cinnamon, nutmeg and ginger in a large bowl, and beat together. Gradually add the eggs, cream, orange juice and zest, beating constantly. Divide the mixture between the pastry shells.

5 Bake for 1 hour. Allow to cool and serve decorated with rosettes of whipped cream.

Serves 12
Preparation time: 25 minutes
Cooking time: 1 hour

CHILLED PUMPKIN PIE

1 x Shortcrust Pastry (see page 34)
1–2 tablespoons orange marmalade
1 ½ cups Pumpkin Purée (see page 34)
2 tablespoons light molasses
⅔ cup firmly packed light brown sugar
½ teaspoon salt
2 teaspoons ground cinnamon
1 teaspoon ground ginger
4 eggs, lightly beaten
¾ cup heavy cream
½ cup evaporated milk
sweetened whipped cream flavored with brandy (optional), to serve

1 Preheat the oven to 400°F.

2 Roll out the pastry on a lightly floured surface and use to line a 9-inch pie plate. Prick the pastry shell all over with a fork, then line it with crumpled kitchen foil weighed down with dried beans or baking beans. Bake for 12 minutes, then remove the foil and beans, and brush the pastry with a thin coating of marmalade. Bake 8 minutes more or until the pastry is set and golden brown. Set aside to cool.

3 Combine the pumpkin purée, molasses, brown sugar, salt, spices, eggs, cream and evaporated milk in the top of a double boiler over simmering water; make sure the top part does not touch the water. Cook for 25–30 minutes, stirring constantly, until the mixture is quite thick and the spoon leaves a deep trail in it; it will thicken only a little more when chilled.

4 Pour the mixture in the baked pastry shell and spread out evenly. Refrigerate 2–4 hours until set. If liked serve with sweetened whipped cream flavored with brandy.

Serves 6–8
Preparation time: 20 minutes
Cooking time: 40–45 minutes plus refrigeration time

PUMPKIN CHEESECAKE

Base:
2 cups crushed graham crackers
½ cup melted butter
2 tablespoons cocoa powder, sifted
2 tablespoons light brown sugar

Filling:
3 cups firmly packed cream cheese
3 eggs, beaten
½ cup sugar
2 tablespoons all-purpose flour, sifted
I cup Pumpkin Purée (see page 34)
2–3 tablespoons finely grated orange zest

Topping:
I cup sour cream
2 tablespoons sugar

To Decorate:
I orange
½ cup sugar
3 tablespoons water

1 Preheat the oven to 375°F. Grease an 8-inch springform cake pan and set aside.

2 Put all the ingredients for the base in a bowl and mix until well combined. Press into the prepared cake pan about 1-inch up the sides. Bake for 10 minutes, then leave to cool slightly.

3 Put the cheese, eggs, sugar, flour, pumpkin purée and orange zest in a bowl and beat together until well combined. Pour the mixture onto the biscuit base. Bake for about 45 minutes until almost set and lightly golden at the edges.

4 Mix the sour cream and sugar together and carefully spoon on top of the cheesecake. Return to the oven for 5 minutes, then turn off the oven and leave the cheesecake in the oven to cool. Chill the cheesecake in the refrigerator for at least 12 hours before removing from the cake pan.

5 Carefully pare the zest from the orange, making sure none of the white pith is attached, and cut it into very thin strips. Place the sugar and water into a saucepan and bring to a boil, stirring until the sugar has dissolved. Add the orange zest and boil for 2–3 minutes until syrupy. Using a slotted spoon, transfer the orange zest to a plate and leave to cool. Sprinkle over the cheesecake to serve.

Serves 6
Preparation time: 20 minutes
Cooking time: about 1 hour plus refrigeration time

TURKISH PUMPKIN TART

1 x Shortcrust Pastry (see page 34)
1 ½ cups Pumpkin Purée (see page 34)
⅓ cup firmly packed light brown sugar
1 tablespoon lemon juice
½ teaspoon ground cinnamon
½ teaspoon ground ginger
2 eggs, beaten
⅔ cup light cream
½ cup chopped walnuts
whipped cream, to serve

1 Preheat the oven to 400°F.

2 Roll out the pastry on a lightly floured surface and use to line an 8-inch tart pan. Prick the pastry shell all over with a fork, then line it with crumpled kitchen foil weighed down with dried beans or baking beans. Place on a baking sheet and bake for 15 minutes, then remove the foil and beans, and bake for 5 minutes more.

3 Put the pumpkin purée in a bowl and stir in the sugar, lemon juice, spices, eggs, cream and half the nuts. Spoon the mixture into the pastry shell and smooth the surface.

4 Reduce the oven temperature to 350°F and bake the tart for 30 minutes or until set. Sprinkle the remaining nuts on top and serve with whipped cream.

Serves 6
Preparation time: 30 minutes
Cooking time: 50 minutes

PUMPKIN PIE WITH NUTS AND RAISINS

1 x Shortcrust Pastry (see page 34)
1 ¼ cups Pumpkin Purée (see page 34)
½ teaspoon ground cinnamon
¼ teaspoon ground ginger
½ cup firmly packed dark brown sugar
3 eggs
2 tablespoons brandy
¾ cup plain yogurt
2 tablespoons raisins
3 tablespoons chopped pecans or walnuts

1 Preheat the oven to 375°F.

2 Roll out the pastry on a lightly floured surface and use to line a fluted, loose-bottomed 9-inch tart pan.

3 Put the pumpkin purée, spices and sugar in a large bowl and beat until smooth. Beat in the eggs, brandy, yogurt, raisins and half the nuts. Pour the mixture into the pastry shell and sprinkle the remaining nuts on top.

4 Bake for 45-50 minutes until the filling is set and the pastry is pale golden. Serve warm.

Serves 6–8
Preparation time: 25 minutes
Cooking time: 45–50 minutes

HALLOWEEN PUMPKIN COOKIES

2 ¼ cups all-purpose flour
¼ teaspoon ground cinnamon
¼ teaspoon ground ginger
¼ teaspoon ground nutmeg
a pinch of salt
¾ cup butter, at room temperature
½ cup firmly packed light brown sugar
2–3 tablespoons finely grated orange zest
½ cup Pumpkin Purée (see page 34)
I egg yolk, beaten

Decoration:
4 cups confectioner's sugar, tightly packed
4 egg whites
I teaspoon fresh lemon juice
orange and black food coloring

1 Sift the flour, cinnamon, ginger, nutmeg and salt together into a large bowl.

2 In a separate bowl cream together the butter, sugar and orange zest until soft and pale. Add this to the flour mixture with the pumpkin purée and egg yolk, and mix to form a soft dough. Wrap in plastic wrap and refrigerate for 30 minutes.

3 Preheat the oven to 375°F. Divide the dough into 2 pieces. Roll out each piece on a lightly floured surface until ⅛-inch thick. Stamp out Halloween shapes of cats, pumpkins and owls with cookie cutters, rerolling any trimmings as necessary.

4 Place on a greased cookie sheet and bake for 10–15 minutes or until light golden. Transfer to a wire rack to cool. When cool, store in an airtight container.

5 For the decoration, sift the confectioner's sugar into a medium bowl. Add the egg whites and lemon juice and blend until smooth. Place half in a separate bowl. Add orange food coloring to the icing in one bowl, and black food colouring to the icing in the other bowl, and mix until well combined. Drizzle or pipe the icing onto the cookies in patterns of your choice.

Makes 50 cookies
Preparation time: 40 minutes
Cooking time: 10–15 minutes a batch

SPICY PUMPKIN TART

Pastry:
1 ½ cups whole-wheat flour
1 teaspoon ground mixed spice
⅓ cup butter or margarine, diced
2 tablespoons light brown sugar
2 tablespoons cold water

Filling:
4 tablespoons mincemeat
2 eggs, beaten
1 ½ cups Pumpkin Purée (see page 34)
⅓ cup sugar
1 teaspoon ground mixed spice
⅔ cup heavy cream

1 Preheat the oven to 375°F.

2 To make the pastry, sift the flour and spice into a bowl, add the butter or margarine and rub in with your fingertips until the mixture resembles fine bread crumbs. Stir in the sugar and water, and mix to a firm dough.

3 Turn the dough out onto a lightly floured surface and knead briefly. Roll out and use to line a 9-inch fluted tart pan. Chill, then prick all over with a fork, line with crumpled kitchen foil weighed down with dried beans or baking beans, and bake for 15 minutes. Remove the foil and beans, and replace the pastry in the oven for 10 minutes.

4 Cover the pastry base with the mincemeat. Beat the eggs, pumpkin purée, sugar, spice and 3 tablespoons of the cream together in a bowl. Pour the mixture into the pastry shell and bake for 20–25 minutes until set.

5 Set aside until cool, then whip the remaining cream and pipe swirls around the edge, and serve.

Serves 6–8
Preparation time: 25 minutes plus chilling time
Cooking time: 40–45 minutes

PUMPKIN SPICE CAKE

½ **cup butter, softened**
1 ¼ **cups sugar**
2 **eggs**
2 ¼ **cups self-rising flour**
½ **teaspoon salt**
1 **teaspoon ground cinnamon**
1 **teaspoon ground ginger**
1 **teaspoon ground nutmeg**
¼ **teaspoon ground cloves**
¾ **cup milk**
1 **cup Pumpkin Purée (see page 34)**
½ **teaspoon baking soda**
½ **cup chopped walnuts**

Caramel Frosting:
½ **cup butter**
1 **cup firmly packed dark brown sugar**
¼ **cup hot milk**
about 3 **cups confectioners' sugar, sifted**

1 Preheat the oven to 350°F. Grease a 9-inch cake pan and line the bottom.

2 Cream the butter and sugar together in a bowl until light and fluffy, then beat in the eggs 1 at a time.

3 In a separate bowl sift together the flour, salt and spices. In a third bowl combine the milk with the pumpkin purée and the baking soda.

4 Add the flour and pumpkin mixtures alternately to the creamed mixture, making sure each addition is well blended before adding the next. Stir in the nuts.

5 Scrape into the prepared pan and bake for 50–55 minutes, or until a skewer inserted into the center comes out clean. Cool the cake in the pan for a few minutes, then turn out onto a wire rack to finish cooling.

6 To make the frosting, melt the butter in a saucepan, add the brown sugar and stir until boiling. Cook, stirring, for 1 minute or until slightly thickened. Cool for 15 minutes, then beat in the milk until the mixture is smooth. Stir in enough confectioners' sugar to give a spreading consistency. Spread on the cake with a flat-bladed knife or palette knife.

Serves 6–8
Preparation time: 20 minutes
Cooking time: 1 hour

PUMPKIN AND RAISIN MUFFINS

2 cups all-purpose flour
2 teaspoons baking powder
¼ teaspoon baking soda
½ cup firmly packed light brown sugar
½ teaspoon salt
¼ teaspoon ground cinnamon
¼ teaspoon ground nutmeg
½ cup raisins
I cup Pumpkin Purée (see page 34)
2 eggs
½ cup milk
¼ cup melted butter

1 Preheat the oven to 400°F. Butter a muffin tin.
2 Sift the flour, baking powder, baking soda, brown sugar, salt, cinnamon and nutmeg together into a large bowl. Stir in the raisins and set aside.
3 Put the pumpkin purée in a separate bowl and beat in the eggs, milk and butter. Fold into the flour mixture until the batter is just combined.
4 Divide the batter among 12 muffin cups (make in 2 batches if necessary), filling each one about two-thirds full. Bake in the middle of the oven for 25–30 minutes until well risen and golden brown, and a skewer inserted into the center comes out clean. Leave in the tin for 1–2 minutes and then transfer to a wire rack to finish cooling.

Makes 12
Preparation time: 10 minutes
Cooking time: 30 minutes a batch

PUMPKIN, ZUCCHINI AND PARMESAN MUFFINS

2 cups all-purpose flour
1 teaspoon baking powder
½ teaspoon baking soda
1 teaspoon salt
¼ teaspoon nutmeg
1 cup shredded zucchini
1 cup Pumpkin Purée (see page 34)
1 large egg, beaten
½ cup milk
¼ cup melted butter
½ cup finely grated fresh Parmesan cheese

1 Preheat the oven to 400°F. Butter a muffin tin.
2 Sift the flour, baking powder, baking soda, salt and nutmeg together into a large bowl. Stir in the zucchini.
3 Put the pumpkin purée in a separate bowl and beat in the eggs, milk, butter and two-thirds of the Parmesan. Fold into the flour mixture until the batter is just combined.
4 Divide the batter among 12 muffin cups (make in 2 batches if necessary), and sprinkle each one with some of the remaining Parmesan. Bake in the middle of the oven for 25–30 minutes until well risen and golden brown, and a skewer inserted into the center comes out clean. Leave in the tin for 1–2 minutes and then transfer to a wire rack to finish cooling.

Makes 12
Preparation time: 15 minutes
Cooking time: 30 minutes a batch

PUMPKIN ICE CREAM

2 cups milk
2-inch piece cinnamon stick
½ teaspoon ground allspice
6 egg yolks
¾ cup firmly packed light brown sugar
2 ½ cups heavy cream
4 cups Pumpkin Purée (see page 34)
3 tablespoons finely chopped stem ginger
(optional)

1 Place the milk, cinnamon stick and allspice in a saucepan, bring to just below boiling point, remove from the heat, cover and let stand for 30 minutes to infuse, then discard the cinnamon stick.
2 Whisk the egg yolks and sugar in a bowl until thick and creamy, and the whisk leaves a trail when lifted. Pour the infused milk into the egg mixture, stirring well. Pour into a clean saucepan and cook gently, stirring constantly until the mixture thickens and coats the back of the spoon: do not allow it to boil or it will separate. Remove the mixture from the heat and pour through a fine strainer into a clean bowl. Set aside to cool, stirring occasionally to prevent a skin from forming.
3 When the mixture is cool, stir in the cream, pumpkin purée and chopped ginger, if using, and chill in the refrigerator for at least 3 hours, or overnight if time allows.
4 Place the bowl in the freezer for 1 hour until the mixture is firm 1-inch around the edge. Whisk well to break down the ice crystals, then return the bowl to the freezer until it is semi-frozen. Whisk again, then freeze until firm. Alternatively, pour the chilled mixture into an ice-cream machine and churn until thick, then transfer to a rigid container and freeze until firm.

Serves 8
Preparation time: 10 minutes plus chilling and infusion time
Cooking time: 10 minutes

SPICED PUMPKIN BREAD

I lb pumpkin, peeled, seeded and chopped
4 cups whole-wheat flour
½ teaspoon salt
½ teaspoon ground ginger
½ teaspoon ground cinnamon
a pinch of grated nutmeg
I tablespoon easy-blend dry yeast
⅔ cup tepid milk
I egg, beaten, to glaze
2 tablespoons chopped
mixed nuts, to decorate

I Steam the pumpkin for 25–30 minutes until it is soft. Press it through a strainer or purée in a blender or food processor. Set aside to cool slightly.

2 Sift the flour, salt, ginger, cinnamon and grated nutmeg into a large bowl and tip in any bran remaining in the sifter. Stir in the dry yeast. Beat in the pumpkin purée and the tepid milk, and mix to a firm dough.

3 Turn the dough out onto a lightly floured surface and knead about 10 minutes, until it is smooth and elastic.

4 Place the dough in a plastic bag and leave in a warm place for about 1 hour, or until it has doubled in size.

5 Knead the dough again for 5 minutes. Divide it into 2 pieces, one twice the size of the other. Press the greased handle of a wooden spoon down through the center of the 2 pieces of dough to join them together. Withdraw the spoon handle.

6 Place the dough on a baking sheet, cover and leave in a warm place to rise for 20–25 minutes.

7 Preheat the oven to 400°F. Brush the top with beaten egg and then scatter the chopped nuts on it. Bake the loaf for 55 minutes–1 hour, until it sounds hollow when tapped. Cool on a wire rack.

Makes a 2-lb loaf
Preparation time: 1 hour, plus 1 ½ hours rising
Cooking time: 1 ½ hours

WINTER VEGETABLE PLATTER WITH ROUILLE

This seasonal dish will look most attractive if all the vegetables are cut into pieces of a similar size, a selection of winter vegetables, such as pumpkin, potato, parsnips, kohlrabi, leek, Jerusalem artichokes, carrots and celeriac are ideal.

extra-virgin olive oil
coarse sea salt
sprigs of fresh herbs, to garnish

Rouille:
I red bell pepper, seeded and chopped
2 garlic cloves, chopped
2 red chilies, seeded and chopped
6 tablespoons extra-virgin olive oil
½ cup fresh white bread crumbs
salt
freshly ground black pepper

I Prepare the rouille first. Put the red bell pepper, garlic, chilies and olive oil in a blender or food processor and combine until fairly smooth. Clean down the sides of the container with a spatula occasionally to ensure all the ingredients are evenly blended. Add the bread crumbs, and salt and pepper to taste, and process again to form a thick paste. Transfer to a small bowl, cover and refrigerate until ready to serve.
2 Prepare the vegetables according to size and type, then boil or steam them until just tender. Drain and refresh under cold running water, the drain again thoroughly.
3 Arrange the vegetables on a large serving platter. Drizzle with olive oil, sprinkle with sea salt and garnish with sprigs of fresh herbs. Serve warm with the rouille.

Serves 4–6
Preparation time: 30 minutes
Cooking time: 20–30 minutes

SPICED SEEDS

I ½ tablespoons corn oil
½ cup hulled pumpkin seeds
½ cup hulled sunflower seeds
¼ cup pine nuts
I teaspoon chili powder
salt

I Heat the oil in a heavy frying pan over moderate heat, then add the pumpkin and sunflower seeds and the pine nuts. Fry, stirring constantly, until all are a rich golden brown. Be prepared for the seeds to pop and jump.
2 Sprinkle the seeds with the chili powder, and salt to taste, and mix well.
3 Tip the seed mixture onto paper towels to drain. Serve warm or cold. Store in an airtight container.

Serves 6–8
Preparation time: 10 minutes
Cooking time: 10 minutes

PUMPKIN AND TOMATO PURÉE WITH MINT

This refreshing purée is especially good served cold with fish, chicken or veal.

¼ cup butter
2 lb pumpkin, peeled, seeded and thickly sliced
½ lb tomatoes, skinned
3 tablespoons fresh chopped mint
salt
freshly ground black pepper

1 Heat the butter in a frying pan. Add the pumpkin slices, cover and cook gently for 8–10 minutes until just soft. Cool slightly.
2 Place the tomatoes in a blender or food processor with the cooked pumpkin and the chopped mint, and purée. Add salt and pepper to taste.
3 Reheat for a hot vegetable dish, or chill and serve ice cold.

Serves 4
Preparation time: 12 minutes
Cooking time: 12 minutes

PUMPKIN CHUTNEY

1 ½ cups vinegar
2 teaspoons mixed pickling spice, or equal quantities of stick cinnamon, allspice berries, whole cloves, mace and peppercorns
1 ½ lb pumpkin, peeled, seeded and cubed
½ lb ripe tomatoes, skinned and chopped
1 cup chopped onions
⅔ cup golden raisins
1 tablespoon finely grated orange zest
2 cups sugar
1 teaspoon ground cinnamon
½ cup chopped pecan nuts

1 Pour the vinegar into a saucepan, add the pickling spice and boil for 5 minutes. Leave to cool, then strain.

2 Put all the remaining ingredients except the pecans in a large saucepan and heat gently, stirring, until the sugar has dissolved. Simmer until thickened, then stir in the nuts.

3 To sterilize a 1-quart glass preserving jar, wash the jar in detergent and water, then boil in water for 10 minutes. Dry upside-down in a warm oven. It should still be hot when you are filling it. Sterilize the lid by dipping in boiling water.

4 Pour the cooked chutney into the sterilized jar and seal.

Note: use the pressure canning cooking method for the best results (see page 7).

Makes 1 quart
Preparation time: 15 minutes
Cooking time: 1 ¾–2 hours

PUMPKIN AND ONION RELISH

2 cups white wine vinegar
⅛ cup sugar
1 ½ teaspoons salt
1 ½ teaspoons black peppercorns
2 tablespoons cold water
1 lb pumpkin, peeled, seeded and cut into cubes
1 cup pearl onions

1 Put the vinegar, sugar, salt, peppercorns and water into a saucepan, bring to the boil and simmer for 5 minutes.

2 Add the pumpkin and onions, and bring back to a simmer, stirring. Simmer for 20–30 minutes or until the pumpkin is just tender, stirring occasionally.

3 Meanwhile, wash a 1-pint glass preserving jar and then boil in water for 10 minutes. Dry upside-down in a warm oven. It should still be warm when you are filling it. Sterilize the lid by dipping in boiling water.

4 Pour the relish into the sterilized jar and seal.

Note: use the pressure canning cooking method for the best results (see page 7).

Makes 1 pint
Preparation time: 10 minutes
Cooking time: 25–35 minutes

PUMPKIN AND GINGER JAM

This jam has a strong ginger flavor. For a less pronounced taste, use a smaller amount of crystallized ginger.

6 lb pumpkin, peeled, seeded and cut into chunks
¾ cup lemon juice
2 tablespoons grated lemon zest
1 cup crystallized ginger, finely chopped
1 tablespoon ground ginger
6 lb sugar

1 Boil or steam the pumpkin until tender. Drain well and mash.

2 Put the mashed pumpkin in a large pot with the lemon juice, lemon zest, crystallized ginger and ground ginger. Bring to a simmer. Add the sugar and stir until dissolved.

3 Bring to a boil and boil for 20 minutes, stirring occasionally as the pulp thickens.

4 Meanwhile, wash some glass preserving jars and then boil them in water for 10 minutes. Dry upside-down in a warm oven. They should still be warm when you are filling them. Sterilize the lids by dipping in boiling water.

5 To test the jam to see if it is set, drop a small amount onto a cold saucer. Place in the refrigerator briefly. The jam has reached setting point if it remains in place when cooled. Then pour the jam into warm jars and seal.

Note: use the pressure canning cooking method for the best results (see page 7).

Makes 6 ½ quarts
Preparation time: 10 minutes
Cooking time: 25 minutes

SAVORY PUMPKIN PURÉE

2 ½ lb pumpkin, peeled,
seeded and thinly sliced
6 shallots or green onions, thinly sliced
I tablespoon water (optional)
a pinch of grated nutmeg
I tablespoon butter
salt
freshly ground black pepper
I tablespoon heavy cream
paprika, to garnish

I Put half the pumpkin slices in the bottom of a saucepan. Put the shallot or green onion slices on top and cover with the remaining pumpkin. Cover the pot, putting a clean dish towel under the lid to make a tighter fit, and cook for 5 minutes over a moderate heat (be careful that the towel does not hang over the pot near the source of the heat), shaking constantly to prevent sticking. The water can be added at this stage if necessary.

2 Reduce the heat and cook for 20 minutes more until the vegetables are tender.

3 Mash well, blend in the nutmeg, butter, and salt and pepper to taste. Heat through again and stir in the cream just before serving. Garnish with a sprinkling of paprika

Serves 4
Preparation time: 10 minutes
Cooking time: 25 minutes

PUMPKIN WITH BACON

Try this delicious dish with roast pork.

2 lb pumpkin, peeled, seeded and
cut into chunks
4 slices bacon, chopped
salt
freshly ground black pepper
grated nutmeg
2 tablespoons milk or light cream

I Steam the pumpkin chunks 15–20 minutes until tender. Meanwhile, fry the bacon in its own fat until crisp.

2 Place the pumpkin in a saucepan, add the fat from the bacon and mash to a pulp.

3 Stir in the bacon, season with salt, pepper and nutmeg to taste. Add the milk or cream, stir and heat through. Serve hot.

Serves 4
Preparation time: 10 minutes
Cooking time: 25 minutes

CANDIED PUMPKIN

2 ¼ cups sugar
⅓ cup water
1 lb pumpkin, peeled, seeded and cubed
colored sugar crystals (optional)

1 Place 2 cups of sugar and the water in a saucepan, and heat gently, stirring, until the sugar has dissolved. Add the pumpkin cubes and cook for 10–15 minutes until just tender.

2 Remove the pumpkin with a slotted spoon and reserve. Boil the remaining liquid until it has reduced by half. Pour the syrup into a bowl, add the pumpkin, cover, and set aside for 6 hours.

3 Place a wire rack over a baking sheet. Drain the pumpkin, reserving the syrup, and place on the wire rack. Coat the pumpkin with the remaining syrup every hour until all the syrup is used. Leave the pumpkin in a warm place for 24 hours to dry.

4 Toss the pumpkin cubes in the remaining sugar or, for extra sparkle, in colored sugar crystals.

5 Pack into small boxes, tie with ribbon or string and label. The candied pumpkin will keep for 2 weeks.

Makes 1 lb
Preparation time: 30 minutes, plus 6 hours marinating, and overnight drying
Cooking time: 10–15 minutes

INDEX